AF522506

KASTURBA GANDHI
A COMPLETE BIOGRAPHY

A. K. GANDHI

Published by
PRABHAT PRAKASHAN PVT. LTD.
4/19 Asaf Ali Road,
New Delhi-110002 (INDIA)
e-mail: prabhatbooks@gmail.com

ISBN 978-93-5521-685-4
KASTURBA GANDHI: A COMPLETE BIOGRAPHY
by A. K. Gandhi

Edition
2025

Price
₹ 300 (Rupees Three Hundred Only)

Printed at
R-Tech Offset Printers, Delhi

Dedicated to
The Women Power of India
who are known for their
love, affection and strength of renunciation.

Author's Note

Kasturbai or Kasturba was on born on 11 April, 1869 at Porbandar. Her biography enables us to get a clear glimpse into the soul of a girl, who from the tender age of thirteen to her death played a pivotal role during the years of freedom struggle in India. Her life was intricately fused with that of Gandhiji. She walked shoulder to shoulder with him in jails and during the racial discrimination movement in South Africa. Her popularity was humongous and Gandhiji once said about her that:

"Those people who came into close contact with me and Ba, many among them had more faith in Ba than in me."

Her role in Gandhiji's life was of a seed from which the massive banyan tree grew, but remained hidden under the soil.

Ba's marriage with Gandhiji at the age of thirteen never seemed like that of a simpatico married couple as simple egoism of childhood often led to sour relations between them. Gandhiji was quite sullen at her illiteracy. He even taunted her sometimes but as they reached the age of maturity, their sentiments started to pass in harmony. Gandhiji introduced her to reading and writing. His influential personality gradually bloomed into Ba's life. As a result, Gandhiji laid down the principles and Ba implemented them in word and deed.

Kasturbai breathed her last on 22 February, 1944 in a prison.

In addition, this would be no exaggeration to say that the glorious life story of this great woman of India would continue to lead and light the coming generations for ages to come.

With this faith and belief…

Contents

Birth and Marriage

"A terrific quality of Ba was to assimilate into me quite spontaneously. I didn't know if this quality was innate to her. However, as my public life brightened up, Ba bloomed, and with her potent views, went on to increasingly assimilate in me, that is in my work, like never before."

—Mahatma Gandhi

A popular adage says that there is a woman behind every successful man. This appears to be literally true when it comes to Kasturba who adopted all the edicts, right or wrong of Gandhiji, and played a vital role in transforming Gandhi into Mahatma Gandhi. A distinctive quality of Ba was that she was never submissive and subservient but still she compromised with Gandhiji's strict, disciplinarian, despotic, staunch, unswerving and abnormal individualistic leadership. Bapu has himself stated, "It is only Ba who tolerates so much. It is tough to spend life with a man like me. Had there been any other woman than Ba, it would have been quite impossible to get along."

Birth

Kasturba was an epitome of mercy, compassion and affection. She was born on 11 April, 1869 at Porbandar in Gujarat. Her father was Gokuldas Makanji, an ordinary trader. Her mother, Vrajkunwar was an ideal homemaker. Apart from her parents, Ba's family consisted of three brothers and a sister. Of these, two brothers and a sister did not live long. Thus, there were only two siblings in the family – Kasturba and her younger brother, Madhav Das.

Education

Ba had distinctive noble qualities and traits of Vaishnava religious faith which she inherited from her parents. However, there was a shortcoming in her charismatic personality. Illiteracy troubled her throughout her life.

She was suppressed by the orthodox contemporary society of the Kathiawar region, where the girls were not sent to school. Gandhiji tried to educate her but with not much success at times he even taunted her for being an illiterate.

Marriage

Ba's father, Gokuldas Makanji was a friend of Karamchand or 'Kaba', Gandhiji's father. To transform this friendship into family relationship, the two decided to wed Ba with Mohandas.

Those days, child marriage was a common practice in many parts of India, including the Saurashtra region. Therefore, nobody raised eyebrows when seven-year-old Ba, older than her future husband by about six months, was betrothed to Mohandas.

The two were married at the age of thirteen in 1883. At that nascent age, betrothal and marriage ceremonies seemed like some celebration of festival to both of them. Gandhiji has discussed this in his autobiography *My Experiments with Truth* that he does not remember whether he was asked for the marriage before betrothal or at the time of wedding. Only the ongoing preparations revealed to him that he was being married. Everything was fine and fascinating, and he himself was quite curious to marry. In his words, "It was only through these preparations that we got warning of the coming event. I do not think it meant to me anything more than the prospect of good clothes to wear, drum-beating, marriage processions, rich dinners and a strange girl to play with."

Mohandas Gandhiji tried as much as he could to pass most of his time with Ba after marriage but because of his large, orthodox joint family attached to social traditions, it was impossible for him to give time to Ba. Only at night was it possible for him to spend time with her. On this anguish, he has expressed, "I wanted to make my wife an ideal wife. My ambition was to make her live a pure life, learn what I learn, and identify her life and thought with those of mine. I do not know whether Kasturba had any such ambition. She was illiterate. By nature, she was simple, independent, persevering and, with me at least, reticent. She was not impatient of her ignorance and I do not recollect my studies having ever spurred her to go in for a similar adventure. I fancy, therefore, that my ambition was all one-sided. My passion was entirely centred on one woman, and I wanted it to be reciprocated. But even if there were no reciprocity, it could not be all unrelieved misery because there was active love on one side at least."

Thus, his desire to teach Ba could not take a concrete form at any turn of life. Describing this mental conflict, Gandhiji has written in his biography: "First the teaching had to be done against her will, and it can only take place at solitary hours of night. In the presence of the elders, I could not even look at her. Therefore, talking to her was out of question. Kathiawar had then, and to a certain extent has even today in its own peculiar, useless and meaningless Purdah. Circumstances to teach were, thus, unfavourable. I must, therefore, confess that most of my efforts to instruct

Kasturbai in our youth were unsuccessful. And when I awoke from the sleep of lust, I had already launched forth into public life, which did not leave me much spare time. I failed likewise to instruct her through private tutors. As a result, Kasturbai can now with difficulty write simple letters and understand simple Gujarati. I am sure that, had my love for her not been tainted with absolute lust, she would have been a learned lady today; for I could then have conquered her dislike for studies. I know that nothing is impossible for pure love."

❑

Ba's Domestic Life

"Those people who came into close contact with me and Ba, many among them had a lot more faith in Ba than in me"

—Mahatma Gandhi

The domestic life of Ba was like a crown of thorns. After marriage, her life was confined within the four walls of the house. Though her mother-in-law, Putlibai, had a special liking for her but life was never serene. Gandhiji was often sullen over her illiteracy and, at times, deliberately poked fun at her. Her make-up, dressing up and stepping out of the four walls of the house often used to make him jealous and suspicious. Furthermore, because of her husband's illness, Putlibai had to spend most of her time in looking after him. The responsibility of the entire household was on

Kasturba's shoulders, which, after the death of her father-in-law, increased even more.

Due to these circumstances, Gandhiji and Ba were always at a distance. In her husband's home, her mother's words often haunted her, "Your back will bend down working at the in-laws' home."

During her first pregnancy, Ba had a rough time and had to endure a lot. Owing to physical weakness, she lost her first child, and somehow recovered enough to lead normal life. Though the household activities kept her busy, but deep inside her, she always felt the torment. The nights were spent in weeping and days in work. There was no one who would listen to her emotional anguish.

Vow of Monogamy

During the initial period of marital life, Ba and Bapu often indulged in innocent clashes. On several occasions, they did not to talk to each other for several days.

One day Bapu read in an article that it is the solemn duty of a husband to abide by the vow of monogamy and was profoundly impressed by this article. It germinated an idea in his psyche – if a husband had to abide by monogamy, then his wife too would be duty-bound to abide by this vow. This idea turned him into a jealous husband. Soon, he changed his stance from 'ought to abide' to 'get it abided by'.

In this context, Gandhiji has written: "When I arrived at the conclusion of 'get it abided by', I inferred that I must keep a watch over my wife. I had no reason to doubt the purity of my wife, but jealousy seldom looks into the cause. I ought to know where my wife goes, so she cannot go out without my consent. This became a source of conflict between the two of us. Not being able to go anywhere without my consent was like confinement. However, Kasturba was none too timid to bear with this confinement. If she wished to go somewhere, she went there for sure without asking me. The more I stressed, the more freedom she attained, and it only irritated me."

In the beginning, men are often motivated to prove their importance and ownership. However, women are generally forbearing and patient by nature. It is due to these qualities on their part that the ship doesn't sink. In his autobiography, Bapu has written: "The canker of suspicion was rooted out only when I understood Ahimsa (or nonviolence) in all its bearings. I saw then the glory of Brahmacharya (or celibacy or self-restraint) and realised that the wife is not the husband's bonded slave, but his companion and his help-mate, and an equal partner in all his joys and sorrows – as free as the husband to choose her own path. Whenever I think of those dark days of doubts and suspicions, I am filled with hatred because of my foolishness and my lustful cruelty…"

Prudence to Make Good from Bad

Despite being illiterate, Ba was prudently learned in discerning good from bad. She confronted evil forcefully, and did not even hesitate to apprise Gandhiji of his follies. Once in the company of evil friends, when Gandhiji started to consume meat, she could not remain silent. To awaken his conscience, she discussed the issue with him soberly and pointed out the good and bad aspects of it. In the end, she even warned Gandhiji that all this was bad for the honour of his family.

Acknowledging her wisdom later, Gandhiji wrote how he, a proud husband, could give in to his wife's commands.

❑

An Effigy of Care

"Ba possesses a trait in abundant amount, which is disproportionate in many other Hindu women. She has found meaningfulness of life in walking after me, out of like or dislike, out of learning or ignorance; and never checked me from living a pure life. Due to this, despite a great divide between our intellect and ability, I always felt that our life was contented, happy and ascending."

—Mahatma Gandhi

After the demise of Karamchand, Ba's father-in-law, Putlibai, Ba's mother-in-law, became detached from all worldly affairs. Separation from her husband turned her into a solemn and serious lady. While Putlibai was in pain after Kasturba was aggrieved at her husband's activities.

In the meantime, Gandhiji had passed high school. It was determined by the elderly members, especially by his uncle and elder brother, that he should become a barrister and choose it as a future course and profession.

Education in the field of law in those days was available only in England. Gandhi decided to go to England for his studies. However, this decision left Kasturba quite sad and worried. Firstly, she was perturbed that in India, Gandhiji had fallen into evil company despite all the controls at home. He ate meat, and he himself admitted before everybody of selling a piece of a gold bangle to repay a debt. Secondly, in a foreign land, there would be none to check him or keep a watch over him, and he would be free from all controls there. Would he be able to exercise control? Kasturba was very anxious about such crucial questions but there was none who could understand her sentiments.

Putlibai, her mother-in-law, after her husband's death was now a detached lady. She took little interest in family and worldly affairs and was mostly absorbed in religious chores. But still she was able to read the lines of despair on Ba's face.

One day, in the morning, when Putlibai was in the prayer room, Mohandas came there to bow before God. She asked him to wait a while, and said, "Mohan, just come here."

"Yes, Mother," saying this, Mohandas sat before her.

“I have heard that you are going to England to study law. Is this true?”

“If you elderly people take this decision and approve my going, it would be a matter of great happiness for me.”

“Can one become a good man there?”

“Yes, Mother, if one qualifies the examination there, a lot of glory and prestige can be earned. It can lead to a good profession, and our days can look up.”

“You can go if you think so,” said Putlibai in a detached voice. “However, you ought not to give up our family’s Vaishnavite traits. I bind you to vow not to be intimate with any other woman and not touch meat or wine. I bind you to this vow.”

Kasturba was in the next room listening to this discourse. She was happy that her mother-in-law had placed before her husband all that she wished. She thanked God and prayed for her husband’s bright future.

Mohandas left for England on 4 September, 1888. Ba was nineteen years old at that time. He took leave from everybody but there is no detail that he also met Ba. From Ba’s point it is, of course, certain that Ba would not have liked his going away without meeting her, or at the most, she could have asked, “When will you response?” and, in return, Bapu would have assured her.

Mohandas was studying in England when his mother Putlibai breathed her last. This also eclipsed Ba’s life into still heavier household duties and busy schedule. There was hardly any time for her to realise when or how the day passed. The wife of Mohandas’s elder brother kept herself busy in worship for hours. Therefore, all duties of bathing children and sending them to school, cooking, washing clothes and other sundry domestic affairs fell into the hands of Ba. Along with the load of household work now, her second child, Harilal, born just a few days before Gandhiji left for England, also became her responsibility.

❑

The Invaluable Gem

"I could not have risen so high if I had not the company of Ba with me. It was she who stood by me through thick and thin; else only God knows, what could have happened. The way my wife shook my inner-self, no other woman in the world could do it. She was my invaluable gem."

—Mahatma Gandhi

Mohandas returned to India in September 1891, after a three-year-long sojourn in England. Now, he was a barrister. His face glowed with a novel passion. His heart was filled with vigour and energy; his youthful heart was bent upon achieving something great in life.

Ba hoped that her husband, Mohandas would admire her for having borne all the massive household duties well. However, unexpectedly, just the opposite happened. He wanted to see his wife literate. He felt let down by his wife's illiteracy. Therefore, he bought her books and a slate in order to instruct her himself. However, only books and slate could not have educated her, for Ba seldom found time for education from her busy schedule.

One day, Mohandas was quite sullen and said, "You are stupid. Education cannot be your cup of tea. I cannot live with a wife like you."

Kasturba grew peevish. She retorted, "Then let me go to my parents, here lies your household." She left for her parental house in a sudden decision.

Mohandas was greatly elated, thinking that the thorn lying in his path had cleared off itself, but soon he realised his mistake. The entire household work came to a grinding halt. Every issue in the house started to take an ugly turn. It reminded him of Ba's lineaments, her model of excellence; a diamond whose value he started to realise after losing her.

Later, Kasturba returned to her in-laws when Mohandas pleaded before his father-in-law, Gokuldas Makanji. This incident dropped their differences considerably.

Recollecting this incident, Gandhiji wrote later: "My interference and doubts fostered in every matter. Due to this, I could not realise all that I aspired for. I had thought of instructing my wife, but my lust did not allow me to attain this goal, and I blamed my wife for all these pitfalls on my part. There was a time when I sent her to her parental house, and accepted to bring her back after giving her a lot of pain. Later, I could realise that all this was utter childishness on my part."

❑

Ba's Sojourn at Bombay

"Bapu's footmarks are embossed on the annals of India's and world's history. Behind these footmarks and in its infinite bottom lies the image of Ba. Bapu and Ba were indistinguishable; they provided energy to each other; they were complementary to each other. Without each other, they could not have risen to such an exalted position, which led to providing a glorious heritage to India and the world."

—G. Ramachandran

On return from England, Mohandas thought of himself as a great scholar of law. He now thought that success would by itself kiss his feet. However, his illusion did not last long. His practice could not bring any worthwhile returns. He thought of trying his hand in Bombay, and shifted to Girgaon, a town of Bombay, with his wife Ba and son Harilal.

The house rent in a large city like Bombay was high. He barely pulled along in his domestic life. Contrary to his ambition and thinking, his legal practice did not show any positive results. However, Kasturba found some solace in this life of pressing needs and her husband's complete company. Moreover, Mohandas' nature was undergoing a phase of transformation. He was no more inclined to split hairs on every issue. He was focussed on his profession but as it became a difficult proposition to survive in Bombay, he moved to Rajkot.

After the death of Gandhiji's father, Mohandas' elder brother Lakshmidas, had become the diwan of Rajkot estate. Mohandas did not like his elder brother, who being a diwan indulged in malpractices in the functioning of the estate. His principles to speak out the truth, however bitter it was, did not straddle him from revealing his sentiments to his elder brother. There was a commotion every time when all the family members gathered. Ba was always worried about her husband. She has seen Gandhiji's failure in law owing to his principle of speaking the truth. She prayed each day for placid atmosphere in the house and better livelihood of her husband. Meanwhile, Lakshmidas' idea to send his staunch brother out of the town for the stake of tranquillity in the family failed. Gandhiji was steadfast in his resolution.

❑

Ba's Journey to Africa

"It is a difficult proposition to say anything in brief so far as Ba is concerned, and nor would it be justice to her. It would be inadequate to say that she was like Seeta, Savitri, Arundhati or Yashodhara; nor can we say that she was like Shardamani, the wife of Ramakrishna Paramhans. History might repeat itself, but personalities are not repeated. Kasturba was unique for many reasons and her life was vital for the extraordinary life of Gandhiji in more than one way, which led to make him a prophet of the twentieth century."

—Ranganath Diwakar

Gandhiji attended court at Rajkot regularly, but it was beyond his capacity to make his practice flourish. He was engaged in his own thinking. He said only what was true, and did what he liked best.

One day, his elder brother said to him, "There is a vacancy for a barrister in the firm of Abdul Karim, a jeweller in Africa. They will pay you a handsome travelling allowance and living expenses in addition to a large salary. Can you go there?"

Gandhiji thought for a while and then consented. All the family members, including Kasturba, heaved a great sigh of relief. However, she was a little anxious over his strange disposition – whether he would be able to stay in a foreign country or not.

Gandhiji has written that he did not feel the pangs of separation while going to Africa as he had felt when he had left for England. In his own words: "While starting for South Africa, I did not feel the wrench of separation, which I had experienced when leaving for England. My mother was now no more… This time, I only felt the pang of parting with my wife. Another baby had been born to us since my return from England. Our love could not yet be called free from lust, but it was getting gradually purer. Since my return from Europe, we had lived very little together; and as I had now become her teacher, however indifferent, and helped her to make certain reforms, we both felt the necessity of being more together, if only to continue the reforms. But the attraction of South Africa rendered the separation bearable."

Mohandas left for South Africa in April 1893. He loved the place so much that he went on to stay there for three years instead of one. Ba passed these three years remembering her husband and serving the entire household.

It was during his sojourn at South Africa that Gandhiji decided to take his family there too, as he liked the place and environment. Therefore, in 1896, he returned to India and, with this, Kasturba busied herself in making preparations to leave for Africa.

Harilal and Manilal were yet infants. A lot of things were needed for them – dresses, shoes, socks, forks, knives, some strange dresses and, God knows, what else. Kasturba did all that Gandhiji said; rather she was bound to follow all that. There was no space for saying 'no'. Doing anything of her free will simply meant to annoy Gandhiji, which she least wanted.

Finally, on 30 November, 1896, Kasturba with her two innocent sons Harilal and Manilal, who anxiously waited for the day, and with Gandhiji, boarded the ship. Kasturba was apprehensive of the complicated circumstances that could prevail abroad: Will we get any known people there? How will I pass the time there? There were numerous questions of this type clouding her mind. She was even inclined to think that some marvel would happen and the ship would anchor back at Bombay. However, this thought never materialised, and the ship didn't stop before it touched the shore at Durban port. Of course, it did face a storm during the voyage. It was so massive that the entire ship shook terribly while the waves lashed at it furiously. The passengers could do little but pray to God for their safety. There were a few anxious moments when it seemed that the ship would go down to the bottomless ocean; but the fervent prayers on the part of the passengers seemed to have rescued the ship out of this monstrous tempest; and they all reached their destination safely.

❑

Ba in Africa

"If I could express my love and sentiments for my wife, I could also express my love and sentiments about Hinduism. My wife influences me more than any other woman in the world."

—Mahatma Gandhi

The ship reached the shore, but none of the passengers was allowed to land. Some passengers whispered that they were being prevented from landing owing to this Gandhi. 'He is the bone of contention behind our holding up,' whispers floated in the ship.

When Ba heard this, she was shaken to the core. She was hard-pressed to understand what the matter was.

The rest of the passengers were allowed to leave the ship

on the third day. Ba and children too were allowed to leave along with Baba Rustamji, a Gujarati friend of Gandhiji. However, Gandhiji was retained there as a threat to his life was claimed.

In fact, those days Africa was burning in the fire of racial discrimination. The white treated the black and the coloured people like slaves. A large number of Indians lived in Africa. Before leaving for India, Gandhiji had delivered a few speeches on this issue. These speeches were published in Africa exaggerating certain facts. As a result, the white people of Durban grew peevish. It was also rumoured that Gandhiji had returned from India with a large number of Indians, and wanted to fill South Africa with the black Indians. Owing to this, many agitated white people waited outside the port to attack him.

The ship's captain was apprised by the government officials that there was a threat to Gandhiji's life. Therefore, he and his family should be allowed to leave the ship only by midnight.

Gandhiji and some of his friends loathed this idea of entering the town like thieves or cowards. In the end, it was decided that Ba and children should accompany Rustamji, while Gandhiji would enter the town in broad daylight, undeterred by threats of death.

And this was what was precisely done.

Mohandas started to walk towards his residence along with a white friend and some other people. When the opponents came to know of this development, they arrived on the scene promptly and started to throw stones and eggs at hm. Kicks and blows with fists followed. The police saved his life somehow, and took him home in a semi-conscious condition.

A neighbourhood doctor treated him. This situation confused Ba and the children badly. However, the trouble had not yet mitigated fully. The whites surrounded the house and started to raise slogans: "Send Gandhi out or we will burn down the house."

The police superintendent somehow got Gandhiji's dress changed to rescue him out. By this time, the crowd had turned out of control but when they could not find Gandhiji despite a thorough search of the house, they dispersed.

Gandhiji returned home four days later, when the matter pacified fully. Until his return, Kasturba continuously prayed for his well-being. She had never envisaged that she would come across such a terrible and bitter experience right on arrival.

Gradually, the circumstances resumed normalcy and Gandhiji's legal practice picked up. He was growing popular owing to his tendency to help the large population of Indians in South Africa.

Ba too started to assimilate herself in the new environment. She felt as if the Divine was influenced by her prayers but her daydream did not last long.

Later, Gandhiji penned down in his autobiography the emotional experiences at Durban. In his own words: "The period (about 1898) I practised law in Durban, my subordinates often stayed with me. They comprised Hindus and Christians, and if I speak province-wise, they came from Gujarat and Madras. I do not remember if at any time I had any sense of discrimination against them. I accepted them all as members of my family, and if my wife ever complained, I argued with her. One of my subordinates was a Christian whose parents came from the Panchak race (a low-caste community). Our house was made in a western style, with no drains in rooms and they ought not to be there too, so I thought. It was for this reason that there used to be a pot for urine in each room in place of a drain, and no servant was assigned to clean that pot. We, husband and wife, shared this responsibility together. Of course, the subordinates who considered themselves as family members started to clean their pots themselves. This subordinate from the Panchak race was new, and we had to clean his pot too. Kasturba cleaned the pots of all others, but she found it unbearable to pick up the pot of this gentleman. It led to some animosity between us. If I picked up his pot, she could not bear it either, and it was quite impossible for her to clean it. She would look at me and say all sorts of things as she climbed down the stairs with the pot. I can still visualise Kasturba climbing down the stairs with those sentiments clearly penetrating her eyes.

"I was an ardent lover but also a harsh husband. I considered myself her teacher, and out of my blind love for myself, I often troubled her.

"I was never satisfied with her carrying the pot with those sentiments brimming on her face. I wanted her to do this job willingly and with a smile. Therefore, I raised my voice and said, 'This cannot go on in my household'.

"This pinched her like a sharp arrow. She retorted, 'Have your house to yourself, here I go'.

"I seemed to have forgotten God. I had not an iota of mercy in me. I caught hold of her hand. The exit door was just in front of the staircase. I drew that fragile and infirm lady to the door and opened the door.

"Her eyes streamed down like the Ganga and Yamuna, and she said, 'You are not ashamed of your action, but I am. Where could I have gone from here? I don't have even my parents here that I could go to them. I am only a woman. So, I would have to bear your thrashing even. Now, feel ashamed and shut the door. It would be insulting if somebody saw us in this state.'

"I retained my angry posture, but felt ashamed at heart. I shut the door. If my wife could not quit me, I too could not have quit her, I had no one else to go to. We quarrelled with each other many times, but the outcome has always been positive. My wife has always conquered over me by her extraordinary forbearance."

Such incidents took place during the initial stage in Africa, and Ba continued to remain an image of tolerance, and endeavoured hard to adapt herself in the new environment.

❑

Satyagraha in Africa

"Whenever we undertook a long and hard travel, Bapu used to say, 'It is Ba who defeats us all. Is there anyone else with so little luggage and so few needs? I exhort for simplicity, still my luggage is double that of Ba.' Despite all of our conscious efforts, we could not stand before Ba's natural, but perfectly clean and glorious simplicity in any measure. Of the entire team, she had the smallest bedding, and her little box was never disorderly."

—Mirabehn

In 1913, the South African government issued an ordinance to hurt the people other than Christians under which all marriages not registered with the court, were illegal.

Gandhiji delivered this news to Ba and said that now their marriage was no more legal, and they would have to undergo a registered marriage.

At this, Ba raged in fury. The husband and wife argued hotly and for long. She opposed the law forcefully. Gandhiji tried to scare her of a jail term, but she was determined for a struggle against the new law.

To challenge the anti-people law of the South African government, Ba prepared to undertake Satyagraha against them. She united and motivated thousands of women coming from Hindu, Muslim, Christian, Parsi, rich and poor segments in solidarity and even went to jail with them.

In the jail, there was no question of partaking the poor-quality vegetable and chapat. Ba refused to eat all that and demanded fruits. When her demand was turned down, she started fasting. The government bowed before her four days later, when she was given three bananas, four pears, two tomatoes and two lemons as only fruits to eat.

Keeping her body and soul together thus, when Ba was released three months later, she looked like a skeleton, suffering from swelling. She underwent medical treatment but to no avail. At this, Gandhiji started his native treatment. He made Ba fast and partake neem, and nursed her by body and spirit.

He would get Ba to brush her teeth with the neem twig, feed her, clean her pot, make coffee for her, and make her lie down in sun the whole day. At times, he even massaged her head with oil and combed her hair into a braid.

This service led to a magnificent and wonderful effect, and Ba could get rid of her illness. This Satyagraha popularised Ba among the local populace.

With the passage of time, the husband and wife continued to face suffering and pains, obstructions and ailments, but they kept coming closer. It is rightly said that hard times bring even enemies close together, and here they were man and wife solemnised into a spiritual bond. Now, Gandhiji had spontaneous love for Ba, and she started to like this new kind of disposition on his part.

❑

Ba's Family

"Ba's bottomless compassion has inherent in it endless fire; her fire is dormant within the cool waters of the ocean. You may or may not believe this mythological legend, yet the ocean of compassion has power enough to destroy sorrow and evil of humanity; and this doubtless fact was adequately manifested by Ba and Bapu in good measure."

—Prabhudas Gandhi

In 1905, Gandhiji practised law in Johannesburg. He lived in a bungalow-type house in a middle-class colony. This two-storeyed house was well-ventilated with a lot of open space. In this house lived Gandhiji, Ba and their three sons: Manilal (11 years), Ramdas (9 years) and Devdas (6 years). His eldest son Harilal (17 years) was in India at this time.

In addition, there lived with them Mr. and Mrs. Polak, an English youth, and some native relatives of Gandhiji among others.

The grain was pulverised at home for food. The task of turning the chakki (hand-operated mill) to grind flour was carried by all the male members, which exercised their limbs quite thoroughly.

Bapu was fond of receiving guests; so, there were 10 to 15 guests at his dining table almost on a daily basis. Ba herself looked after the kitchen. Meals commonly comprised two-three vegetables, dal (pulses), curry, chapati and chutney, etc.

All food was kept on the table so that there was no need to rise repeatedly to fetch or serve food nor did this system require the services of a servant. It was common for the dining table to witness light talk, jokes and laughter.

Later, Bapu delineated this background in his autobiography. He says "Whatever amount of simplicity practicable at a barrister's house in need, was there, but still there were some things without which we could not run work. True simplicity originated from the heart. We grew fond of working ourselves, and started to inculcate these qualities in children too.

In place of buying chapatis from the market, we started to bake yeast-less chapatis by hand at home. The flour from water mill did not work well. Also, it was ensured to use the hand-grounded flour in place of buying water mill-ground flour, because the former is healthier, simpler and thrifty. In view of this, a hand-operated mill was bought for 7 pounds. The stone-slab of this chakki was heavy, and two persons could operate it quite easily, though it was quite tiresome for one person. Polak, myself and children especially joined in operating this chakki. We were also joined by Kasturba at times, but she had barely enough time for the kitchen.

There was a servant to clean the household, he lived like a relative in the house, and children shared his work. The committee attendant came to clean the latrine, but we did this work ourselves."

❑

An Image of Simplicity : Ba

"The venerable Ba was an eccentric image of simplicity, renunciation, service and love. I felt all these every moment when I was in her company."

—Prabhavati Jaiprakash Narayan

In the preceding chapters, we have seen that Ba's entire life was contained in hard work, perseverance, self-renunciation and sacrifice. She was married at an early age of thirteen years, and then took over the responsibility of a large family. Moreover, she had to bear with her husband's ideals, principles, struggles and hard penance, jail terms and Satyagraha. These situations led her to adapt herself to unprecedented situations. To prove her worth, she had to undergo many assessments. In her letters to Bapu,

Sarojini Naidu often addressed him as 'tyrant' or 'my dear tyrant'.

Gopal Krishna Gokhale accepted Bapu as his Guru or teacher. Once, in a jovial mood, he remarked to him: "You are a great tyrant. You shower your love from one side and urge pertinacity from the other, and both these together affect the other person so profoundly that the poor man is but helpless to follow in your footsteps and please you somehow."

In South Africa, Ba had to clean the chamber pots of Bapu's guests. It was quite common for her to attend to the sick. When Bapu went to jail in connection with the Satyagraha movement for the black people, Ba partook the same type of food as Bapu was served in jail, which comprised corn pudding and dry bread. She did not even touch milk or butter all this while. She fell ill owing to this, but did not give up her resolve.

Describing Ba's simplicity, Prabhavati Jaiprakash Narayan has written: "She never allowed me to sleep on the ground. If there was no bed available, she would share her bed with me. She would rise early in the morning at four o'clock to sweep all the rooms, arrange warm water for bathing and take a bath after having cleaned the house; and it was then that she woke me up. I always got warm water ready for bathing.

“Ba’s life was satiated with renunciation, service and love. We girls looked after Bapu, and sometimes visited Ba to serve her. At this, she would laugh and say, ‘You would get tired, though I don’t need all this.’ Her speech was permeated with motherly affection. Ba always felt why those girls should suffer for her sake. She carried her ‘chamber pot’ herself even during rains.”

Ba was ever aware of others’ needs even during her illness. She was a religious and faithful lady. She took only fruits on Ekadashi (eleventh day of bright lunar fortnight). She fasted on all Mondays, Somvati Amavasya (moonless night), Poornima (full-moon night), Janmashtami, Shivratri and other festivals. She continued with her fasts even during her illness.

In the initial stages of her life, she believed in untouchability; but later, she adopted the Harijans (low-caste people) like her own people. A Harijan girl named Lakshmi lived with her like a daughter.

Kasturba had never learnt to be displeased with anybody, and if she was ever annoyed, her voice would still remain as sweet as it was otherwise.

Whenever Vallabhbhai Patel, Maulana Abul Kalam Azad, Jawaharlal Nehru, Dr. Rajendra Prasad, Khan Abdul Ghaffar Khan and other leaders visited Gandhiji, they took some time off to be in the company of Ba, and were ever eager to listen to a few words from her.

At Phoenix Ashram in South Africa, servants were often employed in the household of even ordinary traders during their sojourn there. Yet it was Kasturba who did all things by herself.

As a matter of fact, Bapu bought Ba jewellery, fine silk sarees and the like, but looking at her husband's simplicity, she had adapted herself into simple living. Speaking on this topic, she herself said to Gandhiji once, "It was none else but you who bought me all this, yet I haven't used these things. I have seen that you are a pedestrian of quite a distinct path. You have to adorn the garb of sages and saints. How then could I enjoy all these things? Having seen through your mind, I made up my mind too."

In fact, Ba played a vital role in transforming Mohandas into Mahatma and Bapu. Gurudev Rabindranath Tagore has written at one place: "Those days the sages of India were homemakers, because home was no obstacle to the path of emancipation."

Ba never put herself as a hindrance in the path of her husband's emancipation. Rather, she went on to assume and assimilate in herself his vows, ideals and principles, and, thus, emerged as a true life partner by his side.

It was on Gandhiji's insistence that Kasturba gave up drinking coffee, dal (pulse) and salt; but, of course, she never stopped wearing bangles.

She never wished for jewellery, but never removed glass the bangles from her hands. Bapu was often disturbed by these bangles. He tried his best, but Ba refused to take them off them. She said: "You may say anything, but I am not going to remove them."

So far as property was concerned, Ba had a tin box, whose latch was broken. It contained two cotton sarees made from the cotton handspun by Bapu. Ba wished to dispose of her only property thus: "Manuri (Harilal's daughter), after my death, clothe me in one, and the other should be given to Lakshmi, it is she who is eligible to get it."

In 1906, at the prime of his youth, Bapu assumed Brahmacharya or the vow of celibacy (self-restraint), and it was Ba who cooperated with him fully, and thus made a second-to-none sacrifice. In the words of Gandhiji: "The trait of Brahmacharya proved to be more spontaneous to Ba than me. In the beginning, Ba did not realise what this was. I thought of this and she adopted it willingly. As a result, our relationship blossomed into a true friendship. Living with me from 1906, actually from 1901, there was no other thing for Ba to do but join me in my work. She could not have remained isolated from all this. She could not have faced any difficulty in staying separate, but as a woman and wife in the capacity of a friend, she chose to assimilate and drown herself in my work, and took it as her most sacred duty. In this work, Ba gave a compulsory place to my personal service. She never relinquished looking after my convenience to the last breath of her life."

❑

For Each Other

"She (Ba) was always a firmly determined lady, whom I considered adamant during the initial phase of my married life. Owing to her firm will-power, she unknowingly became my Guru in the art of non-violent non-cooperation."

—Mahatma Gandhi

Owing to Satyagraha and fasting, Ba had to suffer from stomach-related ailments. Once she developed bloody piles at Durban. She was hesitant whether she should undergo surgery or not. At her insistence, the surgery was undertaken without administering anaesthesia. It was a painful procedure, but Ba never sighed in pain. Even the doctors were astonished at her firm attitude.

Bapu returned to Johannesburg after the surgery, while Ba continued to stay at the Durban hospital to recuperate. A few days later, however, Bapu was informed that her condition did not improve; rather, it had taken an ugly turn. The doctor sought Gandhiji's consent to serve Ba with mutton soup so that she could recover quickly. Also, the doctor be allowed a free hand in treating her. However, Gandhiji did not approve of this. Rather, he left the decision to Ba. The doctors, on the other hand, in Gandhiji's absence, fed mutton soup as necessitated by Ba's treatment and informed him about the incident much later.

On learning this, Gandhiji immediately took a train to Durban. The doctor argued that he never thought of sins or otherwise when it came to saving a human life, while Gandhiji termed their actions as perfidious.

Gandhiji opposed him in the strongest terms and said that he was ready to bear with the demise of his wife, but would not approve of giving her mutton soup contrary to her wish.

The doctor retorted with the same stress that he would not like a patient to die for want of consent.

Gandhiji intimated the infirm Ba all that had transpired. On listening to this, she preferred death to partaking mutton soup. Ultimately, she was discharged from the hospital even without the doctor's consent.

Ba was reduced to a cadaverous body due to weakness. From the hospital to Durban railway station, Gandhiji carried her in a rickshaw, travelled to Phoenix by train and finally, from there, she was carried in a carriage for over four km from the railway station to the residence.

Back home, it was now time for Bapu's treatment. He served her wholeheartedly. Ba fully recovered with hydrotherapy, only water was used for this purpose. Just as Bapu saved her life through his nursing, much in the same way, Ba too nursed, served and saved Bapu.

Bapu had given up drinking cow or buffalo milk after he came to know that in large cities like Kolkata, these innocent beasts were forced to under go a procedure quiet heartless. It was from this day that he considered milk equal to meat, and stopped its drinking completely.

Once Bapu suffered from dysentery. It did not take more than a day to weaken his otherwise strong body. He did not take any medicine, and recovered from the illness through his own system of medication. However, he was not able to recover his strength owing to lack of nutrition in the form of milk and curd. His doctors and friends advised him to have milk, or in the alternative, mutton soup or eggs. But Gandhiji declined to accept it. How could a person partake of mutton soup or eggs when he had given up milk considering it to be equal to meat?

On another occasion, another doctor asked him to drink milk, but he stuck to his stand that he had given up drinking cow and buffalo milk. Ba was present just there. She said, "You can for sure drink goat milk."

The doctor too supported her advice. It was from this time that Bapu accepted this piece of advice coming from Ba and the doctor, and this was how Ba helped to save Bapu's life.

❑

Non-hoarding

"If Ba possesses bitterness like neem, she has sweetness in abundance too."

—Mahatma Gandhi

When Bapu was about to retrun home from Africa, people associated and acquainted with him there had moist eyes. Parsi Rustamji, Dada Abdullah, Mrs. and Mr. Kallenbach were of the some important people present at Bapu's house. The house was filled with valuable gifts brought by them and other family members. Many farewell meetings were held in his honour.

Bapu too had moist eyes at the goodwill displayed by the people. Bapu was a man of principles. When he saw the many gifts, he said to Ba, "We ought to return all these gifts; the real wealth being love."

"Will it not hurt the people?" Ba protested.

Gandhiji pondered about the gifts the whole night. It was hard to dispose them or keep them. Finally, it was decided that the gifts should be deposited in a bank, and a trust be created in order to use them for public works.

When Ba heard of this plan, she rose and took out a box of jewellery from the gifts, and said, "You can very well make a trust, but I am not going to give my gift."

"No," said Gandhiji firmly, "nobody has any right over these things, neither you, nor I."

"I don't need any jewellery for myself, but there should be some jewellery to adorn the sons' wives."

"If they wished, jewellery would be got made for them. I will fulfil your wish, but this property belongs to others. We cannot exercise our right on them. It is contrary to ethics." And, finally, according to Gandhiji's wish, Parsi Rustamji was appointed as the trustee of all those gifts, dedicated for public works.

His opinion was that a public servant must not accept any personal gifts.

❑

The Mantra for Khadi

"Ba's heart was full to the brim like the infinite ocean, and it melted as soon as she heard of any person's grief. On such occasions, she forgot about even my charm."

—Mahatma Gandhi

On return to India, Bapu built his ashram on the banks of the Sabarmati River in Ahmedabad. It was named Satyagraha. With him the families of Narhari Parekh, Kaka Kalelkar and Mahadev Desai started to live here. The women residing here comprised Raliatbehn (Ba's sister-in-law), Avantibai, Premabai, Durgabehn, Gangabehn and others.

On his return to India, he heard the pitiable condition of the farmers at Champaran in Bihar who were living in poverty because of the heartless atrocities inflicted on them by the white people ruling India.

No farmer or worker had the courage to raise his voice against the brutal white people. So, Gandhiji took upon himself the task of eradicating their cowardice, and encouraging them to fight for their rights.

Ba and Avantibai visited workers' settlements and tried to understand the agony being faced by women there. Their hearts were ripped apart when they came across the terrible sight of poverty and suffering in the settlements.

In workers' families, three or four women shared a single piece of dhoti, that too was not at all in good state. It could be used by one of them only. As a consequence, the other women were forced to shut themselves up in rooms. To come out in the open was impossible. If there visited a person, they would slightly open the door o rtalk from behind the shut doors. Ba faced this situation a number of times. She enquired for this reason, and then an old woman narrated the tale of their woes.

When their tale of agony was told to Bapu, he motivated people to spin cotton and weave cloth themselves at every household. This mantra of khadi was soon adopted by Ba and the other people. However, some women complained that the saree made from khadi was quite heavy (one kilogram or more), and inconvenient to wear. Bapu would say at such a complaint, "The mothers who carry an infant in their womb for nine months ought not to feel this saree any heavier; after all, this is meant to preserve the honour of our country and poor sisters."

Some sisters complained that it was quite troublesome to wash those khadi sarees; at this, Bapu would laugh and say that he would wash them for them. This was how everybody adopted khadi gradually, and with this, the dearth of clothing was tackled.

❑

Mother of the Ashram

"Ba was fond of learning new things. She started her education at the Aga Khan Palace. She tried to learn even badminton and ping-pong. She had started to play carrom quite well, and played it to the end of her life. When she herself was too infirm to play, she would watch Dr. Gilder and Mirabehn, and on such occasions, she would forget about her own illness."

—Sushila Nayyar

Now Gandhiji's ashram was a vibrant place. Kasturba looked after all the inhabitants of the ashram like her own children. When the strict rules formed by Gandhiji became a bit too unbearable, it was Ba who would advocate for some relief before Gandhiji.

The duties of the ashram were shared by all everyone did their duty readily and devotedly.

The kitchen was common for all the people, and only vegetables grown in the ashram were cooked there. Pumpkin, cut into large pieces, was cooked daily, and no salt, spices or oil was used in it. If anybody wished to take any salt, it was granted.

In the ashram, use of spices and oil was limited. The pumpkin cooked in this manner often used to cause giddiness and, at times, stomach-related ailments. Gandhiji was pertinent to the simple food cooked in the ashram. The problems of the inhabitants were overlooked by him. However, Ba knew all this. She discussed the matter with Gandhiji separately. It was after this discussion that the vegetable started to be cooked in some spices and oil, with simplicity still preserved. Spicy vegetable was served to those women who were not at ease with the pumpkin and Gandhiji never shied away from cracking jokes at them. He would say, "Why, how is the vegetable? That saag is quite spicy, isn't it?"

At such times, Ba would favour the women and say, "You too partook pakodas and puranpoli every Sunday, didn't you?"

At this, Bapu would smile charmingly.

Ba would shower her affection on all people in the ashram. It was owing to her that Pt. Motilal and Jawaharlal

Nehru once stayed at the ashram for days. Ba looked after them specifically.

The ashram had a custom for everybody to wash their dishes themselves and put them back at their proper place. Once, a woman visited the ashram. She took her seat near Ba. When everybody had finished their meals, they rose up with their plates. However, the woman had never cleaned pots all her life, and she was quite perturbed at this novel situation. Ba saw through her difficulty, picked up her plate and washed it herself.

The ashram also had a hospital where Bapu served the sick in his own unique way. The sick often received fruits as gifts. The healthy inmates of the ashram were not served fruits. Even when there was abundant supply of fruits in the ashram, the kitchen managers would continue with their miserliness. On such occasions, Ba would ensure that the extra fruits were distributed among the inmates.

Ba would never forget to distribute sweets on the occasions of fasts and festivals. It was owing to her effort that the ashram's dry environment permeated with warmth and sweetness.

❑

Adopted a Harijan Girl

"Whatever I and Ba possessed was meant for everybody. Ba has never complained about this. I take from her whatever I want. I send everybody to Ba. She has always been in agreement for this."

—Mahatma Gandhi

Gandhiji was a staunch opponent of untouchability. He said, "Untouchability is a crime against God and humanity."

He had a number of low-caste friends in Africa. Gandhiji dined with them. He wanted to eradicate the scourge of untouchability and high caste-low caste considerations completely from India.

One day, on the recommendations of Thakkar Bappa, Gandhiji invited a Harijan family to live in the ashram. It comprised of Dudhabhai, his wife Danibehn and a small daughter Lakshmi. In Gandhiji's presence nobody raised any eyebrows nor when Gandhiji was in sight, but talked about the awkward situation when Gandhiji was away. The members of this family were treated like close relatives. If anybody misbehaved with them or criticised them, they would complain to Gandhiji directly, and in turn, Gandhiji would rebuke the offender. It was somewhat bearable when it came to outwardly interaction and show of brotherhood. However, nobody ever liked their sharing of work in the kitchen, like kneading flour or baking chapatis.

It was owing to this opposition that Raliatbehn, Gandhiji's elder sister, left the ashram saying: "I will no more see you now." And she kept her vow until the last breath.

However, with the passage of time all the ashram inmates accepted and adopted the family. Later, the Harijan husband and wife left the ashram owing to their personal compulsions, but Bapu adopted Lakshmi, their daughter, and assigned Ba with the duty of looking after her. Ba came true to this trust, and brought her up like her own daughter.

❑

The Ashram's Routine

"She (Ba) was like a symbol of purity and simplicity of human heart and human mind. Speech fails to describe an individual who himself is not aware where he wanders. Ba was Ba: completely simple, and at the same time, patient and courageous. She never looked at others' shortcomings."

—Goshibehn

The ashram's routine comprised of prayers at four o'clock in the morning. All the people were expected to join in. Ba followed this routine like a vow. Gandhiji had a habit of taking a nap after the prayers, but Ba always busied herself with other chores in the ashram.

Ba often looked after all of Gandhiji's personal needs herself, such as making lemon water, serving honey, heating water for bathing, bringing food or fruits. When Bapu went for a walk in the morning at about seven, Ba availed the time to take a bath, after which the Gita and Ramcharit Manas were recited by her for one hour daily.

Her duty was to take a round of the kitchen after reading the holy scriptures to ensure that everything was in order. If anything wrong or improper was found, she would point it out straightaway or would start to set it right herself.

In the kitchen, if she found any utensil dirty, she would clean it herself and make it shine and arrange it in the proper place. She would store fruits and vegetables such that they would not rot.

She also took special care of the meals served to Gandhiji and special guests. If somebody else was given the responsibility of cooking their food, she would supervise it in order to prevent possibility of any goof-up. She always ensured that chapatis served to Gandhiji were of uniform size and shape, and that they were all uniformly baked. Bapu could always guess that they were made by Ba herself.

At meal times, she would serve food to Bapu and other guests, and then sit by Gandhiji to eat. If she observed any fly or other insect, she would start to use the hand-fan.

When Bapu read the newspaper after meals in his room,

she would massage his soles with ghee in order to maintain his blood pressure. After he went to sleep, she would take rest in her room for some time, and then wash her face before picking up the newspaper to read.

Bapu had taught her some Hindi, English and Gujarati. It gave her workable knowledge. She kept herself abreast with all that was happening in the country as well as what Bapu was doing at a particular time by reading Vandemataram, Gujarat Samachar and the weekly Harijan Bandhu.

It was compulsory for all ashram inmates to spin cotton. Ba was quite regular at this duty. She always led the rest in the ashram, and did not spin only when she was too ill to rise. Proper accounting was maintained to record who spun how much.

At four in the evening, she would prepare Gandhiji's evening meals. At five, when Babu ate his meals, she would sit near him and drink warm milk boiled with Tulsi leaves and black pepper. In the evening, when Bapu would leave for a walk, Kasturba would visit the hospital and pass some time with the sick, after which, she would go for an evening walk, and return with Bapu.

After this routine, the evening prayer was held and the Ramayana was recited. People would sit and talk for a while after the prayers, and then they would all go to sleep.

Ba always massaged Bapu's head with oil before going to sleep and continued with this routine right until her body cooperated.

❑

Life to March

"Like Bapu, Ba too possessed an independent personality. She could identify the truth not only by intellect, but by her inner inspiration also, and took all her decisions independently. It was on the basis of her own force that she could elevate herself to a higher plane. Bapu is so great himself, and he is an ardent devotee of womanhood, he would never compel anybody to march with him."

—Goshibehn

It is said that an individual becomes somewhat mentally deranged at the age of sixty years. However, Ba had not become even a bit lazy and her old age did not cause any symptom of mental derangement. At sixty, she was agile enough to put even the youth to shame.

There was none who could have seen her laze about her time in idleness. Sitting idle was like a punishment to her. Whatever path she took in the ashram, she would set things right with her own hands. If she found a tumbler upside down, she would put it properly. If she found dirt somewhere, she would pick up the broom immediately. If she found clothes dirty, she would wash them without any hesitation.

If she noticed dirt, cobwebs or the like in Bapu's room, she would promptly clean them herself. She never allowed dirt to settle in his room. She would clean and dust all the things that belonged to Bapu, right from his dishes, footwear, and clock to clothes, and arrange all these things at their proper places.

Ba always dressed herself properly, and expected all others to dress well too. She pointed out anybody who was not dressed well. The young girls in the ashram were scared of her because of this nature only.

Ba did all her chores herself. She declined to use a separate or private toilet. Instead she used the public toilet and cleaned her pot herself.

Ba shared her room with three-four girls all the time. She did her tasks herself, like bringing warm water from the kitchen for bathing, cleaning the room, sweeping and other things. She sought others' help only when she was too ill to rise from the bed.

Sometimes, Ba visited her sons too. Her grandchildren also visited the ashram. She looked after them all well with her love and affection. When the ashram was run on public money, Bapu never liked to spend it on the relatives. He resolved the matter by ruling that the visiting relatives would pay for the expenses of their stay in the ashram. Therefore, whenever the relatives were about to leave the ashram, Ba would ask the manager to give them the bill and charge money. Even the money spent on their treatment was charged from the relatives.

There was a gaushala or cowshed in the ashram. One day, the workers working there were struck by some robbers. The workers were too frightened to continue to work there anymore and left the place. At this, Bapu appointed some people along with Ba to work at the gaushala. She reached there the next day with her companions, and settled down to work. Ba too sat at the hand-mill to grind pulses for the cows. Actually, the gaushala manager was confused as to what work he should assign to Ba, but it was she herself who resolved his predicament.

Whenever Ba was scheduled to take part in some meeting, the managers kept the cot and other facilities ready for her convenience, but Ba was cast from a different fabric. She would engage herself in the kitchen, and reach the meeting venue only when the time came for it. In the meeting, she sat among the audience. She never liked to sit on the dais.

Once, in 1941, Ba went to attend a meeting in Maroli. Gandhiji and other ashram inmates were waiting for her return. There was also a lady waiting to meet her specifically. When Ba did not get down from the morning train, they thought that she would come by the evening train, and informed this fact to Gandhiji. At this, he said, "If Ba belongs to the rich and the moneyed people, she would arrive by this train, else she would come by the Taptivelli via Surat tomorrow morning."

And he was not wrong either. Ba, in fact, came by the Taptivelli the next morning. This was how Ba continued with her active lifestyle right from the beginning till the end.

❑

A Desperate and Anxious Mother

"How dumb I was when Harilal was in the womb! We will have to face the consequences of what I (Bapu) and you (Ba) did. None else but parents are responsible for such conduct on the part of their children. What we can do now is to be pure. We have already been endeavouring to attain this, and we should be satisfied about this. Our purity is bound to have direct or indirect implication on Harilal too."

—Bapu (in a letter to Ba)

Ba had four sons. Among them Harilal was the eldest one. He was born in 1888, before Gandhiji left for England to study law. Ba was very affectionate towards him, and she had to undergo much mental agony on his account.

Harilal Mohandas Gandhi

When Bapu arrived in Durban, Harilal was nine years old. Proper arrangement for his education could not be made there. Bapu did not want to get his children admitted in the whites' school. He even did not like Christian missionary schools. He was also of the view that it was improper to give him education in India as he would be away from him. Harilal went to school in India for some time. However, when Bapu did not find any positive outcome, he called him back to Durban.

Harilal was quite perturbed at this fact that his father had not made proper arrangement for his education. He had also seen that with his father's cooperation, people like Mr. Rich, Mr. Polak and Sorabji Adajania had studied law and become barristers. He impulsively thought – is he not talented enough for such kind of work!

Ba too wished that her sons should get traditional education, but she could not violate Bapu's ideology.

Finally, Harilal revolted against his father and returned to India. Owing to mental conflicts, he could not move beyond matriculation. At this, he entered some profession. The local relatives got him married to Gulab. Unfortunately, Gulab died untimely, which made Harilal quite desperate, and he adopted an evil path. Ba and Bapu tried their best to bring him on the right course, but to no avail. In 1930, he converted and became a Muslim, and named himself Abdulla. Later, he converted back to Hinduism through Arya Samaj.

Ba wrote a number of letters to him to bring him on the right path. Once she wrote: "I don't understand what I should tell you. For the past few years, I have been urging you to practise self-restraint, but you are going from bad to worse with every passing day.

"This life seems to be getting tough for me. Just think of the agony that you are passing to your parents at the close of their lives."

The desperate mother continued to explain how it was worthy to follow the truthful and right path, but Harilal himself said that he had reached the extreme from where he could not return. Despite this, he continued to possess love and respect for his mother. He kept coming to the ashram to meet her.

Once Ba and Bapu were travelling by train. As and when the train stopped at a station, slogans rent the air: Bapu Ki Jai! "Hail Bapu!" However, when the Jabalpur Mail arrived at the platform at Katni, a new slogan rent the air too: "Mata Kasturba ki Jai (Hail Mother Kasturba)!"

Out of curiosity, Ba peeked outside, and she was astonished to find Harilal standing outside, in rags. He had visited her a few years ago. At that time, he was quite healthy, but this time, he was as thin as a rake. He had lost his front teeth as well. Looking at his terrible condition, she found it hard to enquire anything of him.

Harilal extended his arm to hand over an orange and said: “Ba, take this, I have brought it for you.”

“W…wherefrom have you brought it?” Ba asked in a trembling voice.

“I have begged for it.”

Bapu craned his neck near the window and said, “You haven’t brought anything for me, have you?”

“No, this orange is for Ba. What I wish to tell you is that it is owing to Ba that you have become so great.”

“Of course, I have never denied that. You will go with us now, won’t you?”

“No, I won’t. I have come to see only Ba.”

At this, Bapu resumed his seat.

Harilal once again addressed Ba and said, “Ba, only you must eat this orange, else return it to me.”

“No…no, none other than me will eat it. Just look at

yourself! Have you seen your precarious condition? Just think whose son you are. Why don't you accompany us?"

"Ba, this is no more possible now."

Ba's eyes were streaming tears. Just then, the train gave a whistled and moved ahead.

Suddenly, Ba realised that she had not given Harilal anything. 'I have many fruits with me, while he must be starving,' she thought. By the time she could lay her hands on a few fruits, the train had already left the platform way behind.

She could still hear a slogan being raised in the distance: "Mata Kasturba ki Jai!"

Harilal died of tuberculosis in June 1948.

Manilal Mohandas Gandhi

Manilal was born on 28 October, 1892 in India. He served as editor of The Indian Opinion, a Gujarati-English weekly in Phoenix, Durban. Like his father, he had to serve jail terms in connection with opposition to the British anti-imperialist laws.

He was married to Sushila Mashruwala in 1927. He had two daughters, Sita and Ela and a son, Arun Gandhi. He died in 1956.

Ramdas Gandhi

Ramdas was born in 1897 in South Africa. He took part in the freedom struggle with his father. He was married to Nirmala Devi, and had three children: Sumitra, Kanu and Usha. He died in 1969.

Devdas Gandhi

Ba's youngest son, Devdas was born in 1900 in South Africa. He returned to India with his parents. He took active part in the freedom struggle with Bapu, and went to jail a number of times.

Devdas was a leading journalist too. He served as editor to the Hindustan Times for several years.

Rajaji C. Gopalachari took part in the freedom struggle alongside Gandhiji. His daughter Lakshmi fell in love with Devdas. However, Lakshmi was only fifteen years old while Devdas was 28 at that time. Therefore, Mahatma Gandhi and Rajaji asked them to live in isolation for five years before they could be united. At the end of this period, the two married in 1933 with the consent of Mahatma Gandhi and Rajaji. They had four children including Rajmohan and Gopalkrishna.

Devdas died in 1957.

❑

Community Service at Champaran

"She (Ba) had unprecedented faith in Bapu's decisive intellect. She did not understand politics, but she knew Bapu well. This was enough for her. She reflected the attitude of the millions of trusting Indians."

—**Sushila Nayar**

On returning to India, Ba started her first Satyagraha struggle at Champaran. She was little interested in showing off, and did not like processions and meetings. However, she took active part in constructive service.

As has been described in the earlier, the condition of the

poor workers in Champaran was quite pitiable. Ignorance of education, uncleanliness and diseases was rampant.

Gandhiji started a madrasa at a village called Bhitiharwa, and appointed Ba and some other volunteers to serve there. Ba stayed there and went round the surrounding villages in order to spread awareness about the need for cleanliness and also distributed medicines for minor ailments.

One day, Gandhiji visited a village near Bhitiharwa. He saw some women wrapped in dirty clothes. Bapu asked Ba to motivate them towards cleanliness. Ba spoke to those women. One of them led Ba to her hut and said, "Look, we have nothing but this saree to wrap our bodies with. If Gandhiji helps us with some clothes, we can do all what you wish us to do."

Looking at so much penury in the country, Ba and Bapu cried desperately.

The area faced chilly weather. In the winter season, the hut was covered in frost. Ba, however, continued her community service despite unfavourable conditions and exploitation by the local English officers.

Once when she returned from her assignment of community service, she found her hut completely burnt down. A new hut was constructed the same night, so that her work would not suffer.

The local English officer didn't like Ba's community service. He often issued statements against her to be published in newspapers. He went to the extent of saying: "Smt. Gandhi was there to incite people against the government."

Ba, however, with her slight knowledge of Hindi and Gujarati, little cared for all these newspaper statements, and devoted herself fully to the cause for which she had set out.

❑

Freedom Fighter Ba

"It is evidently obvious from the community service rendered by Ba that no scholarliness is needed to undertake public welfare measures. Rather what is needed is just love for people and to know what right thing ought to be done. In this matter, her insight was quite simple and straight."

—Mahatma Gandhi

Kheda Satyagraha

The situation had not yet improved at Champaran when at Kheda in Gujarat, government officials raided common people and seized all valuable things like jewellery, and many animals. This action had been taken because the lagaan or revenue tax had not been paid. In fact, the people were suffering owing to the already prevailing massive drought conditions. They did not even have enough grains to eat. In such circumstances, they pleaded before the government for some solace and requested the government to cancel lagaan, but their entreaties fell on deaf ears, and action for seizure was taken up.

This inhuman action despaired Ba greatly. She promptly rushed to Kheda. People grew enthusiastic when they found Ba among them. They felt some relief from the wounds that the government had inflicted upon them.

A mass meeting of the women was held there, which Ba addressed:

"Our men have started the struggle for truth against the government, and we ought to encourage them. We must bear with the suffering that the government has inflicted upon us. If they seize our goods, let them take it. If they snatch our land, let them have it. However, under no circumstances, must we pay the tax. When the people tell the government that no crop could be produced, it must trust them . And if the government does not agree and continues with its atrocities, we must not waver from our path at any cost. Never be scared of the government servants. Rather, have patience and encourage your sons and brothers and husbands; give them courage to move ahead."

Listening to this majestic speech, the women rose in vigour. Many of them came forward and assured Ba in these words, "Ba, when you are taking so much of trouble for us even at this age, we will not allow fear to envelop us. We resolve not to pay the tax to the government."

Struggle for Self-rule

Gandhiji was lodged in jail for six years from 1922 following his participation in the freedom struggle. The entire country grieved. Ba too was anxious and desperate. However, she controlled herself and sat down to complete the tasks that were rendered incomplete owing to Gandhiji's imprisonment. She went to places in order to motivate people. Her speeches were vigorous and energetic. She would say:

- "The sentence given to my husband has certainly made me restive, but it could not put me down. I am sure we will get him released through our efforts well before his term expires."
- "Success or failure lies in our hands. I plead with those who love Bapu that they should contribute in taking forward his tasks. They should engage themselves in spinning and weaving cotton."
- "All men and women must give up foreign clothes and use khadi instead, and should encourage others too."
- Spinning of cotton should be taken as a solemn religious duty, and you should motivate all those who live near you."

- "All traders and merchants should give up sale and purchase of foreign clothes."

This exhortation on the part of Ba had a massive positive impact. Bonfires of foreign clothes were organised at many places. Charkha or spinning wheel became an inseparable part of people's lives. People started to take up khadi like never before.

Bapu was shifted from the Sabarmati Jail to Yervada Jail. During this period, Kasturba went from village to village and worked among the tribals. In their company, thousands of tribals gave up drinking and started spinning cotton, and also took to singing religious hymns.

Ba was confident that the truth would prevail ultimately.

—Stri Swaraj Sangh

In 1930, Bapu set out on the historical Dandi March leaving behind some tasks to be accomplished by others, like prohibition and boycott of foreign clothes.

At this time, the Stri Swaraj Sangh (Women Self-rule Association) was formed under the leadership of Ba. At her call, hundreds of women joined this organisation.

Posts were created in towns and villages. It was under the influence of the charming leadership of Ba as well as her inspiring speeches that the liquor-houses in Surat and other places became deserted, which were earlier ill-famed for heavy drinking. The government had to change its policy of governing liquor. It permitted sale of wine and liquor through vendors.

The government also issued a dictum that people should not rent out houses for establishing branches of the Stri Swaraj Sangh. When it became difficult to find places for this purpose, the branches were officiated in tents, and thus they continued to function unabated. At this, the government started to burn down these tents and seize property. Ba was not discouraged. She said at this crucial juncture: “Now we will live in thatched huts and make do with earthen pots.”

Ba was busy with her task when she received the news of Bapu’s arrest. She was unhappy that despite his non-violent protests, Bapu was arrested in the middle of the night.

Addressing the countrymen on this occasion, she said,

“Gandhiji isn’t among us, but we have to continue to tread on the path that he has shown us. He has assigned different tasks to brothers and sisters. Now it becomes our duty/dharma to fulfil them.

“The countrymen should not be agitated by the incidence of Gandhiji’s arrest. Rather, this fire burning within them should be utilised in the non-violent struggle for freedom.”

Issuing an emotional appeal to the government servants, she said, “The policemen lambast and shoot their own countrymen and brethren. What is the use of using violence against innocent and patriotic children when they weep and sigh later? Brothers! Keep courage. God will not keep any of you hungry. Resign from your jobs with faith in God, give up your government jobs."

It was on her exhortation that hundreds of government servants resigned from their jobs. The British inflicted atrocities on them, yet could not break their will.

Encouraging the women, Ba said, "You ought to stand by and encourage the men. When the brothers stand in favour of the selfish government, the sisters should warn them and keep off from cooperating with them, if needed."

Call by Telegram

One day, early in the morning, a telegram was received. It was sent from Borsad.

The farmers' lands were being auctioned because they had not paid the lagaan, and they were being incarcerated as well. When the women refused to pay the tax, they too were dealt with cruelly. Numerous women were admitted in hospital. Ba was then sent in order to eradicate the shadow of terror enveloping the village.

Ba took no time to catch the train and arrived at Borsad.

When she saw the pitiable condition of the women in the hospital, she felt anguished. However, she was happy too as these women had suffered to honour her word, and had undertaken the task assigned by Gandhiji. They had accomplished the task in true spirit.

Ba went around the whole village and motivated the people who found in her visit a healing touch to their agony, and now they started to plan the future course of action.

This hectic schedule fatigued Ba greatly, as lately she was not keeping well. The doctors advised her to take a complete rest, but she had no time for this.

She was now sixty-three years old. She had undergone jail terms several times in 1932 and 1933, which had weakened her physically. Still, she retained her motivation.

Rajkot Satyagraha

In the beginning of the year 1939, Gandhiji visited Bardoli at the call of Sardar Vallabhbhai Patel. There he came to know that the diwan of Rajkot and the government had promised the people several rights and facilities, but had gone back on their promises. At this, Gandhiji started the Satyagraha. Sardar Patel was with him on this occasion. When Ba heard of this, she too joined the struggle. As it was, Rajkot was her own hometown. How could she lag behind when her hometown was under the shadow of grief?

She was arrested at Rajkot on the charges of violation of civil non-cooperation movement, and was kept in a solitary confinement.

When Bapu came to know of her arrest, he started fasting at Rajkot. Troubled by this, the government was forced to release her.

❑

The Final Confinement

"Ba's death seems like a dream. No doubt, I was ready for this, but when she actually went away, I was astonished. It appears that I could not do my personal work well without her."

—Mahatma Gandhi

Ba was gravely ill after the Rajkot Satyagraha, but still she accompanied Gandhiji during his tours of Calcutta, Delhi, Bombay and other places.

On 8 August, 1942, Bapu addressed the All India Congress Committee meeting. Contrary to his expectation, he was arrested at six on the morning of the next day. Ba too presented herself for arrest. At this, Bapu explained to her the situation and said, "You can come if you can't live without me, but I think that you should continue with my work instead of accompanying me."

Hearing these words, Ba stayed back. She was greatly shocked by his arrest, but his words had infused in her a new life even when she was not well.

Bapu was scheduled to deliver a speech in a general meeting at the Shivaji Park in Bombay. In view of his arrest, Ba decided that she herself would address that meeting.

When she was getting ready to leave, she was informed that she would be arrested on the way. As she came out of the house at quarter to five to head for the venue, she found a police officer standing at the door, who folded his hands before her and said, "Mother, you are old enough to take rest at home. Better you don't attend the meeting."

However, Ba was reluctant to abide by his wish, so she was arrested. The other volunteers arrested with her included Dr. Sushila Nayyar and Pyarelal (brother of Dr. Sushila Nayyar).

They were first taken to the Arthur Road Jail in Bombay, and on 11 August, they were shifted to the Aga Khan Palace Jail. Gandhiji was already lodged there.

It was from this jail that Gandhiji took the services of his private secretary, Mahadev Desai, whom he considered like his son, to write letters. He also got a letter written to the

Viceroy requesting him to send Sardar Patel too to the same jail. This made Mahadev Bhai quite happy as he was hopeful that Sardar Patel would keep Gandhiji in good humour in otherwise serious environment of the jail.

The Aga Khan Palace was flies and mosquitoes. Ba kept swaying the hand-fan in order to keep the mosquitoes away from Bapu. It was in the company of Bapu that her physical condition improved somewhat. Now, she had started to walk around and cooperate in the kitchen too.

Distressful Trauma

It was Saturday, the fifteenth of August in 1942. The jail witnessed hectic activities on the part of prisoners as Col. Bhandari, the Inspector General of Jails, was scheduled to visit. The prisoners were busy cleaning the jail.

All of a sudden, Ba and Bapu were informed that Mahadev Bhai had suffered a heart attack. They ran to his room. They found him lying on the cot writhing in pain. Bapu called, "Mahadev, Mahadev!"

Ba called in a pathetic voice, "Mahadev, O Mahadev, Bapu calls you!"

Sadly, Mahadev was no more in this mortal world to answer their call.

Ba loved him like a son. His death shook her completely.

She said, "How unjust God is! He had taken away the son before his mother. Be at peace wherever you may be!"

Bapu's Fast

On 10 February, 1943, Bapu commenced his 21-day fast at the Aga Khan Jail. This period was very painful for Ba. She passed most of her daytime praying to God and sought longevity and success for him.

During this period of twenty-one days, there were many occasions when Bapu lost his consciousness and fell down on the cot. However, his fast came to an end on 3 March, 1943, and no obstacle was faced. During this period, at times, people even gave up any hope for Bapu's life and at such crucial junctures, Ba motivated them by saying that Bapu would not suffer from anything as long as she was all right. And it was the result of her faith and dedication that Bapu's tenacity was accomplished without any hindrance.

❑

Emancipation

"Ba wove herself in the fabric of my life homogeneously/ inseparably. The void created by her departure can never be filled. It is not that I am surrounded by grief, or I am always absorbed in thinking about her. I cannot, in fact, describe my condition in words."

—Mahatma Gandhi

During Gandhiji's fasting, the doors of the Aga Khan Palace were thrown open for the visitors so that people could meet him. This opportunity was also availed by his sons Devdas and Ramdas. Ba was elated to meet them. It appeared as if a new wave of energy coursed in her body. However, when the government noticed that Gandhiji's condition was improving and his life was no more endangered, it stopped visitors from meeting him.

Now, Ba's condition once again started to deteriorate. On 16 March, 1943, her heartbeat shot up suddenly, and she remained in this condition for close to two hours. She underwent such an attack again on 25 March. She started medication this time, and continued right until the end.

She often prayed to get released from the jail. When Gandhiji heard this, he remarked that she had still seven more years to stay in jail. This made her an anxious lady. She was strangely convinced that she was not going to live beyond a few months.

At this juncture, most of Bapu's time passed in correspondence with the government. He invested some of his time in teaching Ba subjects like history, geography, the Bible and the Gita among other things.

At times, Ba felt bad as to why she had not started learning all those things earlier. Bapu taught her names of rivers, names of India's provinces, names of capitals, Gujarati language among other things, but the 74-year-old Ba was sorry that she could not reply to Bapu's questions correctly at that ripe old age.

Rites and Rituals

In the jail, Ba regularly recited the Valmiki Ramayana, Bhagavad Gita and other religious scriptures. Manu too was brought to jail to look after her. Ramayana and other holy texts were also recited by her with their meanings explained.

Ba liked the incidence of Bharat Milap or meeting of Ram and Bharat. She would entreat to recite it again and again. She also recited the Ashram Bhajanavali and the Anasakti Yoga.

Fond of Games

Ba loved the game of carrom very much. In the beginning she used to watch it being played but then she started to try her hand at it, and learnt it well enough. She often felt bad when defeated, so other players often tried to make her win. Whenever she was able to put the coins into the holes, she would clap in a child-like manner to express her elation. If she pocketed the coins regularly enough, she would not even feel bad for her defeat.

She also watched the games of badminton with interest. She played the game of ping-pong until her body could take it.

Bapu's Birthday

It was the second half of 1943. On 2 October, on the occasion of Bapu's birthday, she distributed food among the prisoners with her own hands, and also tried to share work so far as she could, though she was quite weak physically.

Ba had given Manu a khadi saree made by Bapu with an instruction to keep it safe. That day, she wore the same saree, and wished that she may wear the same saree during her final journey.

Growing Illness

From November 1943, Ba wasn't keeping well at all. She had difficulty in breathing if she walked a little. So, she was taken about in a wheel-chair.

By the month of December, her condition deteriorated further and she had to be put on oxygen.

When her condition further went down, the government consented to allow the relatives to meet her. She was immensely happy to meet her two sons – Ramdas Gandhi and Devdas Gandhi, and felt especially peaceful.

One day, Harilal Gandhi also came to meet her, which made her very happy.

In February 1944, Ba remained serious. She was not gaining health despite naturotherapy and medical treatment. In addition to Dr. Sushila Nayyar, there were other doctors like Dr. Dinshaw Mehta, Dr. Gilder, Vaidyaraj Pt. Shiv Sharma, Vaidyaraj Joshi and others, who looked after her, but their treatment helped her only momentarily, and she returned to her grave condition sooner than later.

The British government allowed for her treatment after a lot of negative responses. At times, Gandhiji had to write letters in quite a strict language. He went to the extent of writing thus: "If I am unable to make necessary arrangement for my wife's treatment, then I entreat you to shift me to some other jail, so that I don't have to be a mute and helpless witness to her agony."

Gandhiji's Devotion to His Wife

During Ba's illness, Gandhiji would visit her several times, and would sit by her side on the cot for long.

He looked after her during pneumonia. He would clean Ba's mouth with a handkerchief whenever she discharged phlegm or sputum, and washed it himself. At daytime, whenever he passed by her room, he would collect the dirty handkerchiefs to wash them. If someone wanted to stop him from doing this, he would remark, "Let me do this. I like to do this."

Despite his busy schedule, Bapu always gave Ba one hour daily for cold bath and then a long warm bath. On this, he often said, "I think it is invaluable for me to get the divine chance of serving Ba in the latter half of life."

Just a day before her death, when Ba met Devdas, she said, "Now, it is you who has to look after all the others. Bapu is a sage. He is worried about the entire world except himself. You are well aware of Harilal. Therefore, it is you who has to support the family."

22 February, 1944

Ba looked quite restless on this day. When Bapu went to see her in the morning, she stopped him from going for the morning walk and asked him to be with her. Bapu sat with her till ten o'clock and assured her of her well-being.

At noon, Bapu visited her again and fed her two spoonfuls of Ganga water. Meanwhile, other relatives arrived. They induced strange energy in Ba that brought her in conversation with the relatives.

When she looked at Devdas, she repeated what she said, once before, "You have served me much. Now, it is you who has to support everybody, and continue to do my duty.

Devdas said, "Ba, how have I served you? I have come here just the previous night. These are the people who have served you so well."

After this, she looked at Bapu and said, "There is nothing to grieve over my death, is there? Rather sweets should be distributed on this occasion."

Then she closed her eyes and folded her hands with the words – "O Lord, I have eaten like a beast. Forgive me for all this. Now what I want is your devotion and your love, and nothing else."

In the meantime, a medicine called penicillin was fetched from Calcutta. However, under the prevailing condition, Gandhiji did not think it right to administer it to her.

Evening had approached and Bapu was now preparing to leave for his evening walk. He used to go for the walk at half-past six, but being busy today, he could not go until quarter-past seven. As he was about to set out, Ba called from behind, "Bapuji!"

Bapu came and sat beside her. Kanu wanted to take a photograph but he stopped him.

Ba was feeling restless. She placed her head in Bapu's lap. Bapu started to pat her head softly. Ba started to speak with pauses, "Now I am going off. We have lived a life mixed with pleasure and sorrow. Nobody ought to weep for me. I am tranquil, I am at peace now."

Bapu asked all those present to recite Ramdhun a hymn in praise of Lord Rama. All of them started to sing – Raja Ram Ram Ram, Sita Ram Ram Ram.

Just about this time, Ba took a couple of hiccups, and soon after, gave up this mortal body in the lap of Bapu for all time to come.

Just a couple of days ago, Bapu had uttered, "How can my service be so devoted that Ba would breathe her last in my lap? Only God could know better."

This privilege fell in Bapu's share. The time seemed to have stopped then.

It was thirty-five minutes past seven in the evening. It was the day of Maha-Shivratri. It was the time when the temples were offering evening prayers; bells were ringing. It was on this auspicious occasion that Kasturba gave up her body.

Devdas clung to Ba's body and cried like a child. All people were shocked and sad, sorrowful and bereaved.

Bapu, too, was tearful but then he controlled himself to support Devdas. After all, Bapu was the Father of the Nation. How could he display his sentiments so easily?

Final Rites

The next day, that is, on 23 February, the gates of the Aga Khan Jail were opened for Ba's relatives to visit. Ba was placed a pyre made of sandalwood just near the samadhi of Mahadev Bhai. She was adorned with the same khadi saree that she had droped on the occasion of Bapu's last birthday. Mukhagni or sacred fire was offered by Devdas, after which her body was amalgamated into the five elements. Now, no government could keep her confined any more.

Bapu remained in attendance until four in the evening. He was undergoing a great storm of agony within himself, but tried to look as normal as could be.

Expressing his sentiments on parting with his life partner of over 62 years, Bapu said, “I cannot imagine my life without Ba at my side. I had wished that she set out on her final journey while I am still alive, so that I don’t have to worry about her life after me. She was an inseparable part of my life. The void created by her departure can never be filled.”

Ba’s sacrifice did not go in vain. How long could the government retain the innocent people in jails? Finally, the same year on 6 May, Bapu was released from jail together with all his comrades.

Mother of the Nation: Ba

It was under the care of Ba that Bapu rose to the status of the Father of the Nation. And from this viewpoint, Ba occupied the glorious seat of the Mother of the Nation. Gandhiji himself has admitted on more than one occasion that Ba looked after him like a mother. In fact, Ba never differentiated between her own children and others. It was owing to this liberal attitude that people called her Ba (or mother). Bapu himself addressed her Ba. Who would not have cried at having lost such a mother?

This story of Ba and Bapu may look quite simple to read, but it is woven with sour and sweet experiences of life in a fascinating and complicated manner, quite similar to what we find in mythological tales, that compels the readers to spare a few moments to think over.

There are scarce chances that such a unique personality would ever be born who could raise an ordinary man into the exalted status of Bapu; and in these words lies the true tribute to this great woman of India.

❑

Some Anecdotes

Dislike of Receptions and Celebrations

Ba least liked any outwardly show, receptions and celebrations. Once during a march, some people wanted to pin on her saree a medallion saying, 'Karo ya Maro' (Do or Die). She prevented them from doing this, proclaiming that this slogan was embossed right in her heart.

In 1930, Devdas Gandhi was lodged in the Gujarat Jail. When he was released, Ba went to see him. The local leaders wanted to organise a march under her leadership in order to enthuse the masses but since she hardly took any interest, the plan was postponed. On this occasion, some people were heard saying, "Leaders appreciate such types of marches and processions, why should then Ba disallow us from doing this?"

Inclined to Cleanliness

Ba had a habit to do all her tasks at the definite time. If any person erred in this regard, she would rectify him, expressing it indirectly. She would roll and arrange her bed herself, and place the thick mats properly. She never left any of her tasks half done. If she noticed anything incomplete, she would to do it herself. The utensils in the kitchen shone brightly as if they were new and this was evidence enough of her cleanliness.

Participation in Risk

In 1929, Gandhiji stayed at Kosani for some time. It was the time of extreme winter. Despite heavy and thick fog, Bapu continued to sleep in the open as he was wont to.

One day, some volunteers from Nainital observed a tiger's cub wandering around Bapu. When they brought this to Bapu's notice the next morning, Bapu laughed it out and slept in the open on the next night too. At this, Ba too risked her life by putting her bed outside with Gandhiji's bed.

Bapu's Nervousness

One day, Ba and Bapu went out for a walk like they usually did. Suddenly, Bapu tripped over a piece of stone and his toe started to bleed. Bapu asked Ba to bandage the wound and seemed somewhat nervous. At this, Ba asked, "You are little afraid of death; how then can this small wound baffle you?"

"Ba, this body belongs to the people," Gandhiji said. "If this wound deteriorates, I will not be able to work for a few days, and this would obstruct the work I have undertaken on behalf of the people."

Large-hearted Ba

In 1932, when Bapu undertook a fast in the jail, the government allowed Ba to visit him. However, Ba did not avail the advantages of this permission.

She said, "There are a number of people in the jail; many of them are ill too. When their relatives cannot meet them, how can I? I am just another one of thousands of such wives and mothers. These women too must be equally worried for their husbands and sons."

Ba's Gift

A pupil of Gurudev Rabindranath Tagore visited Sevagram from Shantiniketan. He stayed there for several days and when he was about return, Gandhiji himself came to see him off at the ashram gate. As he was about to step out, somebody called from behind and he turned only to find Ba standing. He went near her and asked, "Ba, do you wish to say something?"

Ba handed him a packet and said, "This may be useful to you during your long journey to Shantiniketan. You might be aware that Bapu likes yeast bread. When you get back to Shantiniketan, just inform me how you liked this."

The motherly treatment filled the pupil with gratitude and he bowed down before her in reverence.

Ba's Memories

A day after Ba's death, a water bottle was kept near Bapu, wrapped in an old cloth in order to keep the water cool.

Seeing that cloth Bapu said, "Tear off a piece of this cloth. Ba frequently used it. So, it is quite valuable for me."

Bapu often used earthen bandages during his naturopathy and he wanted to use that cloth precisely for this purpose.

In Ba's Absence

After Ba's death, Sushilabehn visited Gandhiji from South Africa. She was the wife of Manilal Gandhi and was Bapu's daughter-in-law. During the conversation, she happened to say without much thought, "Bapu, you seem to feel lonely, do you?"

Hearing this, Bapu grew very grave and responded, "Ba was woven into the fabric of my life. There is no doubt that I feel very lonely in her absence."

Ghee Lamp

During their sojourn at Sevagram, Ba lighted a ghee lamp on Bapu's birthday. On this occasion, the ashram inmates and those from outside had also gathered. They all wanted to hear something from Bapu but he kept sitting silently, looking at the lamp constantly. Ba was sitting just next to him. After a long pause Bapu broke the silence and asked, "Who has brought this lamp here?"

"Me," Ba said briefly.

"Wherefrom?" Bapu enquired further.

"From the neighbourhood village," Ba said. "It is your birthday, so I brought it."

Bapu was silent for a few moments and then said in a solemn voice, "Nothing inauspicious would have happened had this ghee lamp not been lighted today. I can see countless poor people around. They don't have even a morsel of food, and here we are lighting a lamp full of ghee in the ashram."

After this, he addressed Ba, "You have been living with me for several years now, but what you seem to have learned is this. How does it matter if it is my birthday today? This day should be marked with good deeds, not by sinful deeds. We must not misuse anything that the poor of the country cannot have."

Ba's Wrath

Ba and Bapu were staying at Maganwadi, Wardha. As a rule, all inmates were duty-bound to undertake all tasks in turn. One day, it was the turn of Bapu and Kumarappa to clean the utensils. On hearing the sound of falling pots and pans, Ba rushed to the kitchen and said, "Gentlemen, don't you have anything else to do? You have a lot of other important tasks to take care of, why don't you then leave this task to others?"

However, Bapu only laughed and continued with his cleaning. This made Ba very angry and she snatched away the pot from Bapu's hand while he still held the coconut scrub.

At this, Bapu remarked humorously, "Kumarappa, you are very fortunate indeed, you don't have a wife to rule over you. I give in to this command from Ba in order to allow peace to prevail in the household, and pardon me, I am leaving Ba as your companion to help you in the work."

After this, Bapu washed his hands and feet and went away, leaving behind Ba and Kumarappa to finish the remaining work.

Ba's Love for Khadi

Once Ba hurt her foot. A volunteer came running with a fine piece of cloth and said, "Ba, this piece of fine and soft cloth will give you more comfort than the rough khadi."

"No, I will use a khadi bandage only," said Ba, "even if it is thick and rough, it would not bite me or make me uncomfortable."

Ba: Mother to All

Just two-three days prior to her death, Ba asked Dr. Gilder for medication of castor oil. However, the doctor disallowed it saying that it could further induce weakness."

"What happens then?" remarked Ba. "Even otherwise I am sure to die now."

"What makes you say so?" Dr. Gilder said softly. "Today Ramdas and Devdas are coming to see you. Don't you want to see them?"

Ba smiled mildly at this and said, “All people here are like my own children. So, any of them can perform the final rites on my death.”

Ba’s Humility

Bapu was away at Cuttack, to take part in the meeting of the Gandhi Seva Sangh. He was accompanied by Ba, Durgabehn, and others Leelawatibehn.

Jagannath Puri was not far from there. Some people chalked out a programme to visit the shrine and Ba went with them. She visited the holy place with all devotion and returned.

In the evening, Bapu came to know of this visit. He said to Ba, “How can we go to a temple where no Harijan is allowed to enter?”

Ba begged foregiveness for her mistake in all humility. At this, Bapu said, “This is none of your mistake. I am your instructor and I seem to have left your instruction midway. What else could you have done?”

In Favour of Hindu-Muslim Unity

Whether in jail or outside, Ba treated all Hindus and Muslims equally. She met Muslim people amiably, such as

Hakim Ajmal Khan, Khan Abdul Ghaffar Khan, Maulana Abul Kalam Azad and others. When she saw their good-heartedness, she grew restless about the atrocities inflicted by the Muslim rulers in the past.

She distributed sweets among Muslims on the occasion of Eid and repeated the gesture on the occasion of Diwali too. She treated all people at the Sabarmati Ashram equally, whether they were Hindus or Muslims.

I Will Not Eat

Ba was a fine cook and was very fond of eating and serving food. However, her heartbeat shot up whenever she ate heavy (oily) food.

One day in the Aga Khan Palace Jail, compelled by a craving for puranpoli (an oily food), she got it cooked and said to Manu, "Go and ask Bapu if he too would eat it."

On the enquiry, Bapu said to Manu, "I can eat only if Ba doesn't."

When Ba came to know of this response, she promptly said, "All right, I will not eat it."

Ba's Nature is Such

One-and-a-half month after Ba's death, Bapu contracted malaria. One day, he said to Dr. Sushila Nayyar, "It is good that I did not contract it before Ba, else she could have put you all in my service."

"You are right, Bapu," said Sushila. "In my view, she would have gone a step further. She would have forgotten her own illness in order to serve and nurse you."

An emotional Bapu said, "Of course, it 'is' her nature to do so."

Immediately he realised his mistake and rectified his statement, "I mean to say, Ba's nature 'was' such."

"But for you, Ba lives even today, she is still alive," added Sushila.

"That too is right," remarked Bapu.

Indifferent World

When Bapu and other national leaders were arrested suddenly in August 1942, Ba was hurt greatly.

She was waiting at the Bombay railway station when she was being taken to stay with Gandhiji in the Yervada Jail. At this time, she said to Dr. Sushila Nayyar, "Look, Sushila, what a festive look it is around, as if nothing has happened. The world continues with its usual activities. How can Bapu bring self-rule if such indifference prevails?"

At this, Sushila said with moist eyes, "Ba, God is with Bapu. Everything will settle down for the better in the end."

Marriage's Memories

One day, Bapu participated in a wedding anniversary function and when he was on his way back to the Sabarmati Ashram, a sister joked with him, "Mahatmaji, didn't you recall your own wedding in this programme?"

Bapu laughed heartily. He had been married at a tender age of thirteen years. He remarked, "Who can forget about his marriage? I still remember that day. The priest was chanting hymns while I and Ba were pressing each other's hands."

Hair in Milk

Bapu was in Aligarh. A person requested Ba that the duty of serving milk to Bapu be handed over to him. When Bapu was served milk, Ba noticed a strand of hair in it and prevented Bapu from drinking it. Bapu asked why she had stopped him, and Ba's explanation only made him angry.

Bapu did not drink milk that day. This made Ba sad. She said, "Bapu, who is in the service of the nation, will have to go hungry today. But what can I do? If I refuse to permit somebody from serving Bapu, he simply feels bad."

In the future, if Ba ever assigned Bapu's service to anybody, she would ensure that everything was well. She personally supervised the task.

Ba's Arrest

Bapu was arrested on the morning of 9 August, 1942, and the same evening Ba too got arrested.

Bapu was lodged in the Aga Khan Jail in Poona, while Ba was taken to the Arthur Road Jail in Bombay.

There Ba contracted dysentery. She was not keeping well, and this ailment further deteriorated her condition.

Later, Ba was also taken to Gandhiji. He was shocked to look at her and remarked, "Did you request the government to stay with me, or has the government done it of its own accord?"

Ba kept silent for a while as she could not understand what Bapu actually meant.

Dr. Sushila Nayyar was present and she informed him that it was the government that had transferred them from Bombay to Poona.

It was only now that Ba could understand what Bapu had tried to mean. She said, "We have been arrested."

At this, Bapu heaved a great sigh of relief.

Ba – Bapu's Mother

Once Bapu visited Sri Lanka with Ba. There some people mistook Ba for his mother. Not only this, she was felicitated and introduced at a public function as Bapu's mother. The convener then turned to Gandhiji and said, "Why didn't you bring Kasturba with you?"

Bapu only smiled mildly in response. Later, in his speech, he said, "Just now a gentleman, who introduced me, has committed a minor mistake. The woman accompanying me is not my mother like he described her, but my wife. But, in a context, he is quite right. Years ago, we both mutually consented to end our relationship as husband and wife, and since that day, I have looked at her as my mother."

Sensitive Ba

Ram Narain Chaudhary was brought to the Sabarmati Ashram for treatment of his skin disease. Bapu started his treatment. He advised Ram Narain to have some currants daily and sent him to Ba. He had not gone more than a few steps when Bapu called him back and said, "You must be ready for some sour experiences there."

Ba did not know Ram Narain. Therefore, as soon as he asked for currants, Ba asked Pyarelal, "Do you know him? He wants the currants that I have kept for Bapu."

Before Pyarelal could say anything, Ram Narain said, "Ba, I am new to this place. I don't know anybody. I do not want it myself, but Bapu has sent me to you for currants."

Ba melted at this and said, "All right, there is nothing to mind. I had a lot of currants with me, but Bapu has got all that distributed among patients. I have kept some currants aside for him, but it appears you need it more than him. Here are the currants for you."

When Ram Narain came to know that Ba was giving him currants from Bapu's share, he was unwilling to take them. At this, Ba stressed and handed him over the currants, and then enquired of his family in all affection.

Ram Narain returned to Gandhiji after some time. Seeing him smiling, Bapu was amazed. However, when he heard what had happened, he said, "Of course, it is only Ba who can be such a lady. She can rage in wrath if she finds any of my shares being diverted, but her heart is like the fathomless ocean, filled to the brim with belongingness. As soon as she looks at others' sufferings, she is filled with compassion to the extent to forget even about me."

You are Scared of Me

At Sabarmati Ashram, Ba was responsible for the kitchen. It was she who looked after the visiting guests. She was assisted by some volunteers in this task.

One day, in the afternoon, she laid down for a brief rest after she had finished her duty in the kitchen. Just then, Pt. Motilal Nehru and some other guests arrived.

As Ba had gone to take rest just a little while ago, Bapu asked one of her assistants and Kusumbehn to cook food for them. He instructed them to seek Ba's help only if it was absolutely necessary. He also asked them to clearn up the kitchen after lunch.

While working in the kitchen, the assistant happened to drop a plate. The sound woke Ba and she rushed to the kitchen, afraid that a cat had entered it.

However, she was amazed to see food being cooked again. She enquired about the need and angrily proclaimed, "Why didn't you inform me?"

The assistant tried to be clever and said, "We were about to call you, but you were taking rest. So we thought of preparing everything before calling you."

"You too were as tired as I was," said Ba. "If you can work again, why can't I?"

After this, she too started working.

After the guests left in the evening, she said to Bapu, "Why should you assign the duty of cooking to the young people? Am I so lazy?"

"Truly speaking, I was scared of telling you for this," said Bapu.

"You are scared of me!" Ba broke into a loud laugh.

❑